Joe Faust

Frank Brennan

Series Editor: Rob Waring

HEINLE
CENGAGE Learning™

Australia • Brazil • Japan • Korea • Mexico • Singapore • Spain • United Kingdom • United States

HEINLE
CENGAGE Learning™

Page Turners Reading Library

Joe Faust
Frank Brennan

Publisher: Andrew Robinson

Executive Editor: Sean Bermingham

Senior Development Editor:
Derek Mackrell

Assistant Editors:
Claire Tan, Sarah Tan

Story Editor: Julian Thomlinson

Series Development Editor:
Sue Leather

Director of Global Marketing:
Ian Martin

Content Project Manager:
Tan Jin Hock

Print Buyer:
Susan Spencer

Layout Design and Illustrations:
Redbean Design Pte Ltd

Cover Illustration: Eric Foenander

Photo Credits:
75 lingbeek/iStockphoto,
76 Wikimedia Commons

ISBN-13: 978-1-4240-1796-6

ISBN-10: 1-4240-1796-3

Heinle
20 Channel Center Street
Boston, Massachusetts 02210
USA

Cengage Learning is a leading provider of customized learning solutions with office locations around the globe, including Singapore, the United Kingdom, Australia, Mexico, Brazil, and Japan. Locate your local office at:
international.cengage.com/region

Cengage Learning products are represented in Canada by Nelson Education, Ltd.

Visit Heinle online at **elt.heinle.com**

Visit our corporate website at
www.cengage.com

Printed in the United States of America
1 2 3 4 5 6 7 – 14 13 12 11 10

Contents

Review

Background Reading

People in the story

Joe Faust
a young trader at a large
Manhattan company

Brad Benson
Joe's boss

Don Smitty
a trader who has just
committed suicide

Dawson Coles
an experienced trader

Bonnie Perez
a young lawyer at Joe's
company,
and Joe's girlfriend

Rey Todd
a mysterious older man at
Joe's company

The story is set in New York City, in the USA.

Chapter 1

An eye for the market

Manhattan, New York City, USA

The streets of Manhattan were busy, as usual. It was a late afternoon in October. Tall buildings stood outlined against a pale blue sky. On the twentieth floor of one of the tall buildings a man stood by an open window.

He looked down at the streets far below.

He took a deep breath.

He jumped.

◇◇◇

Twenty-four hours later, Joe Faust sat at a desk in the same building. He was a few floors down from the twentieth floor. His tie was undone and his face was damp with sweat. I've bought thousands of shares for my clients, he thought, and if that computer screen doesn't show a rise in their price soon, I'm in big trouble!

Joe Faust was a city trader. He bought shares on the Internet for his clients for as low a price as possible, then he sold them for as high a price as possible. He was always looking for a profit. Joe and his company got a percentage of the profits he made for his clients. But Joe had spent all the money he had been allowed on the shares he saw on the screen in front of him. He had been so confident they would make a profit that he had spent even more than he was allowed. Joe knew it was risky. The company didn't like losing money. Not one bit.

5

"Come on! You just have to come up in price!" he shouted at the screen. His hand was held over the computer keyboard. He was ready to push the key that would mean the sale of all the shares he had bought. If the shares went down any more in price, he could lose his job.

At least they didn't go down anymore. But Joe didn't push the key yet. He waited for a few minutes. "Come on!" he shouted. Finally, the shares went up in price. They went up again. And again. And again. Then they stayed still.

"Now!"

Joe pushed down on the key and sold all the thousands of shares he had bought in an instant.

"Yes!" he yelled with delight. "Oh, yes!"

Joe was still laughing to himself when the phone rang. It was his boss, Brad Benson. "Joe, I want you in my office, now!"

I wonder what that's all about, Joe thought to himself as he stood up. He hoped he wasn't in trouble. Even making money could get you into trouble if you didn't play by the rules. Unless, of course, you made enough. Joe fastened his tie and left.

A few minutes later Joe Faust was in the office of his boss, Brad Benson. Brad Benson was sitting behind his oak desk. He was about forty years old. Most of the hair on his head was gone though he did have a thick, brown mustache growing on his upper lip. Joe admired the expensive Italian suit his boss was wearing. He wished he'd put on something better than his sports jacket.

"You did some good trading just now, Joe," said the older man. "But it was risky. Our kind of business has to buy at low prices and sell at high prices. Your shares were bought cheap and looked like they would stay cheap. I don't know how you knew they would go up so much in price. But who cares? You knew and that's all that matters. You have a good eye for the market, Joe. It's getting you noticed!"

"Thank you, Brad," said Joe. It was just what he wanted to hear. "That's what I'm here for—to make bigger profits for us."

"For our clients," Brad Benson corrected him. "Though we, of course, take our percentage. And so do you, Joe—you've earned yourself a generous cash bonus today. The company likes to reward good traders. And you're proving to be one of our best young traders, Joe!"

Joe felt pleased. A bonus! Extra money was always good. He was convinced that he was the best trader in his company. Soon his company would know it, too. Maybe he would get a life contract one of these days. Maybe, for now, he could get the Investem Life Insurance Company account.

"Won't the Investem Life Insurance Company be looking for a new man to look after their business now, Brad?" Joe asked. "How about me? I know I could make a good job of it."

"You mean after Don Smitty made such a bad job of it?" Brad answered. "His death yesterday was most unfortunate—he was one of our top traders. I don't know why he lost control of things so suddenly, but I do know it cost the company a great deal of money. Anyway, we've already given the Investem account to Dawson Coles. He's very experienced and will take good care of it, I'm sure."

"If you say so, Brad," Joe said quietly.

Brad smiled. "Dawson Coles comes from a family of city traders. He has a first-class degree from Harvard and is a highly respected trader himself. He's also been with this company for ten years. You may be the best trader New York has ever seen, Joe, but you still need a little more experience. You've only been with us for one year. Now you keep on doing a good job and one of these days, you may well get your big opportunity. Hey, go out and have a good time. You've earned it."

◇◇◇

There was a hotel in the same building as his office. Joe sat in the hotel bar and ordered a drink before he went home for the evening.

The bar was his usual place to relax after a day's work. The low lights and dark furniture usually helped him to switch off. This evening the beer tasted good as usual, but he couldn't stop thinking about work. I keep doing a good job, he thought, so why don't they give me the jobs I deserve? And why was it always Dawson Coles who got the best jobs? "Dawson Coles!" he suddenly said out loud. His voice was angry. The barman turned around toward Joe, and Joe put his hand up to say "It's OK."

Still, things were improving, thought Joe. Though it wasn't a lot compared to the kind of big cash bonuses Dawson Coles earned, Joe was glad to have made some extra money today. It was quite a few thousand dollars and that wasn't bad at all. No sir. Even Bonnie ought to be impressed.

Bonnie Perez was a young lawyer who sometimes worked for Joe's company. She was pretty with dark hair, brown eyes, and a figure that made men's heads turn. She was smart, too, and was already being recognized as a rising star in the world of business law.

And she was Joe's girlfriend.

Joe wanted to see more of Bonnie but they were both busy people. The few times they were together they had a good time. "Only let's not talk about work and money," Bonnie had told him. "Not when we're together. I get enough of that at work. Let's just be happy being together."

"But my job is all about money!" Joe always protested.

"OK," Bonnie said. "You can talk about it when you've made a bonus of a million dollars at least. Agreed?"

Joe had agreed. After all, they had enough other interests in common—jazz music, good food, and a love of Manhattan. They were young, bright, and in love. That was all they needed.

But, surely, Bonnie wouldn't mind hearing about his bonus. It wasn't a million dollars but it was the biggest bonus he had made so far. Ever since Joe had been a kid in the poorest part of the Bronx he had promised himself that, one day, he would be worth millions of dollars. Bonnie understood that, didn't she?

As Joe picked up his cell phone to call Bonnie's number he stopped, put the phone down, and stared across the bar.

It was Bonnie! She had just walked in, at the other end of the hotel bar. She was laughing with a tall, well-dressed man with short, brown hair. Joe felt his heart thump and his face go hot as he recognized the man.

It was Dawson Coles!

Bonnie saw Joe and smiled in recognition. Joe put down his cell phone and smiled back, trying his best not to show the anger he was feeling. Dawson Coles ignored him. Then, Joe saw Coles take hold of Bonnie's hand and kiss it. Two glasses of champagne arrived. It was probably the most expensive champagne in the place, Joe thought as he looked at his beer. Yes, that's just like Dawson Coles.

But Joe knew that Bonnie often met important clients for a drink. She was used to the kind of attention businessmen sometimes gave to her. This was no different. Joe knew this was strictly business. Still, Joe hated the idea of his girlfriend working for Dawson Coles, of all people! One day he'd be so rich that Bonnie would never have to work for someone like Dawson Coles again.

Joe got up and left to go home.

Outside the building he saw that part of the street was still closed off. It was the place where Don Smitty's body had been found. Police were still investigating his death, but everybody knew that Don Smitty had jumped from the twentieth floor. Joe looked up at the high building. He knew trading was a stressful job and not everybody could take the pressure. But he also knew he wasn't like Don Smitty. He was Joe Faust and he was going right to the top. Yes, sir.

By the time Joe got back to his apartment, had a shower, and put on a suit, he wasn't thinking about Smitty any more. He was going to Macey's Bar.

Chapter 2

Macey's Bar

The New York City lights shone brightly in many colors against the night sky. Joe looked out from his cab, admiring his favorite city.

"Macey's Bar, you say, right?" the cab driver told him. "Here it is."

Joe left a tip for the driver and went into Macey's. It was where many of the young traders went. Joe didn't drink much, just a glass of beer or a soda now and then. But he didn't go there for the beer or the soda—he went to find out what was going on in the world of city trading.

Not everybody kept a clear head like Joe. Sometimes their careless talk gave him tips about trading that he would not have heard otherwise. Joe knew that could give him an advantage at work. There was money to be made out of careless talk.

All the usual people were there. Joe sat where he always sat, at a table in a dark corner close to the bar. It was a small table for two, set apart from the others. Maybe it was meant for private conversations, maybe for lovers. Whatever the reason, it gave him some privacy and was good for listening to people talk without being noticed.

The talk Joe heard tonight was mostly about Don Smitty. People were saying that he was a man who couldn't handle failure. That's why he took a jump from the twentieth floor. He wasn't the first and he probably wouldn't be the last, they said. Joe listened to three traders at a table nearby.

"Look, I told you—the guy had a contract for life and they only give those to the best. Smitty was one of the company's top men, wasn't he?" asked the first trader.

"You mean he used to be before he went downhill," answered the second. "It was real quick, too. He owed millions, they say."

"The guy was supposed to be smart, wasn't he?" a third trader asked. "I thought he handled that Investem Life Insurance account."

"Well, he handled it badly this time all right: he lost control completely," the second trader added. "He cost the company a hell of a lot of money. That's what I heard."

"Yeah, well Dawson Coles made it back for them," the third trader said. "Joe Faust did OK, too. I'm telling you, that Faust kid is really hot. Pity he isn't so well-connected. You know, he could be really big otherwise. But you have to know the right people in this business. What chance does a kid from the Bronx have against somebody like Dawson Coles, huh?"

Joe heard every word and knew it was true. What chance did he have against somebody like Dawson Coles? He needed something to give him an advantage. Joe knew he had the brains to succeed. But you needed more than brains in this business; you needed luck and you needed to know the right people and have the right connections. That's what it took to be rich. Really rich. Joe's ambition burned inside his heart like fire. He would do anything to know the right people, anything for a lucky break, anything to be as rich as Dawson Coles. No, richer. Anything. He took a sip of his drink and looked around the bar.

Sometimes Joe liked to talk to traders he knew. Not tonight. Since seeing Bonnie with Dawson Coles, he felt like being alone. Macey's Bar was a good place to be alone in.

Joe loved New York at night, and Macey's Bar was what New York at night was all about. It was big and played cool jazz music with the lights down low. He took Bonnie there sometimes. Yes, jazz was his favorite, especially when it had slow saxophones, base, and drums, like tonight. Somebody once told him that jazz was called the devil's music but he didn't care. Joe looked at his beer glass and raised it to his lips, whispering, "I like the devil's music!" to himself.

"So do I," said a soft southern voice close to Joe's ear.

Joe almost fell from his seat. He hadn't realized anybody was there.

"I'm sorry, Mr. Faust," said the voice. "I didn't mean to alarm you. I like jazz, too."

Joe turned to see who was speaking. It was a small, middle-aged man in a pale suit. He had a round face and a neat, white beard. He looked friendly, like a favorite uncle. Only Joe didn't have any uncles.

"Hey, how did you hear me?" asked Joe. "I could hardly hear myself—or can you read minds or something?"

The man laughed. "You are mistaken, Joe—may I call you Joe? I heard you quite clearly," and he laughed again. His laughter had a quality about it that cut through the background noise without being loud. It was a laugh that Joe found he couldn't ignore. It made Joe feel relaxed though he wasn't sure if that was the right thing to be.

"Who are you?" Joe asked.

"I'm surprised you haven't seen me here before," the man said. "I come to Macey's Bar quite often. I'm from the company, just like you. I like to listen to what goes on, same as you. My name is Rey Todd."

Macey's Bar.

15

Joe couldn't remember seeing Rey Todd before but there was something familiar about him that he couldn't quite place. Maybe it was the cologne he was wearing; it had a strong, bittersweet smell that reminded Joe of sweet wood smoke. It was probably an expensive cologne, the kind that senior people in the company often wore because it smelled expensive and usually was. Yes, maybe that was it.

"And just what, exactly, do you do at the company, Mr. Todd?" Joe asked.

"I look out for promising young souls," said Todd. "Sometimes we find people with the kind of qualities we're really looking for. Naturally, we don't want to lose men like that. Men like you, Joe."

Joe felt excited. Even so, he didn't want Todd to know it. He wanted to look calm and in control. He smiled and leaned back in his chair.

"Tell me more, Mr. Todd."

"You still don't trust me? Good. I like that!" Rey Todd laughed again. This made Joe feel a little more relaxed, but at the same time, he still felt nervous. It was a strange feeling.

"You have determination, Joe," Todd continued. "You came from a poor part of the city but you still wanted to succeed. You're a good-looking guy—and smart, too. You got yourself an education and promised yourself you would never be poor again. Am I right so far?"

"So far, yeah," Joe answered. He felt a cold feeling run down his back, even though the bar was warm. Yes, Todd knew about him all right. Maybe he was from the company.

"In fact," Todd continued, "you were angry. You're still angry. Why is that, Joe?"

Even as Todd spoke, Joe could feel that his anger was still there.

"Do you mind me being honest, Mr. Todd?" Joe asked.

Todd laughed softly. "Go right ahead, Joe."

"I know I'm good," began Joe. "I know how the market works better than anybody—and I get results. But it's other people who get the important jobs that make the big money. And why? Because they're wealthy graduates from important universities like Harvard who have the right background and know all the right people."

"You mean people like Dawson Coles?" asked Todd.

"Well, yeah!" Joe answered with more feeling than he had wanted to show. "I know he's good, but I know I'm better! I just need a chance to show it."

Todd smiled. "Dawson Coles does know important people, it's true. But now you know somebody important. You know me."

Todd threw a card onto the table.

"The company wants people who are with us all the way, one hundred per cent," Todd said, this time with no laughter. "In return we can offer you all that you asked for."

Joe thought he saw another expression in Todd's smiling face. It was an unpleasant, hungry look that lay beneath his smile. It was gone in a second.

"And just what did I ask for, Mr. Todd?" said Joe.

Todd's round face looked sad for a moment. "Don't play with me, Joe. You want to be rich, don't you? Really rich? Of course you do!"

Joe nodded. Todd was right and they both knew it. Joe felt like his mind was something that Todd could read as easily as reading a book. He didn't like the feeling and found himself looking at the floor before returning his eyes to Todd's smiling face.

"Now I'm going to leave you with a little something to help you," Todd told him, "some advice that's a gift beyond price. You say you know the market? You say you have a real feel for profit? Well, just for the next month follow those feelings; believe in them. Do what those feelings tell you to do and see how far they take you. Let's see if you really do have a feeling for profit, Joe. Profit is our business. We always want more, Joe. Don't ever forget that."

"Are you offering me a promotion, Mr. Todd?" Joe asked.

"Maybe. Just do your work and follow my advice. Impress us, Joe," said Todd with a little laugh. "Come back and see me in one month, and maybe, if we like what we see, we can offer you a special deal."

Somebody broke a glass in the background, and Joe turned around for a moment. When he turned back, Rey Todd had gone. There was no sign of him, just the smell of his bittersweet cologne.

But there was Todd's card on the table. On it, written in gold letters, were the words Rey Todd, Room 113.

Chapter 3

The gift

In the cab home, as he looked at the bright lights of the city night through the windows, Joe thought about Rey Todd's advice. Todd called it his "gift," but surely he was just recognizing Joe's natural ability for making a profit, wasn't he? The more Joe thought about it, the more he felt that he was at last becoming noticed by important people. Rey Todd was an important man in the company, he was certain of that. Joe smiled. He felt good.

He soon reached his small but comfortable apartment on the edge of Manhattan. Property was expensive there, and Joe, though he earned good money, was not rich.

Maybe that was about to change.

Joe was too excited to sleep much that night. He kept thinking about his meeting with Rey Todd. He felt that Todd, more than anybody he had ever met before, understood Joe's hunger for profit. Joe loved winning. He wanted to be rich, yes, but he had a pride in his ability to find profits in the market. It excited his heart more than anything else. He recognized the same thing in Todd. And Todd, he was sure, recognized it in him.

He wouldn't tell Bonnie just yet, he thought. Not until he made his first million dollar bonus.

The next morning, Joe had a quick shower, a hurried breakfast, and left for work. He bought the business paper and read it as he sat on the morning train. A young man with short, blond hair and wearing glasses was sitting next to him. It was Sam Lazlo, a keen young trader Joe knew from the company. Sam looked at the business paper over Joe's shoulder.

"They say coffee prices are going to stay the same for a while," Sam said. "What do you think, Joe?"

Without a moment's hesitation, Joe said, "No way! They'll rise for a couple of days then go back to today's price."

Joe had sounded so sure of himself that Sam said, "Hey, thanks for the tip, Joe!"

Normally, Joe kept his ideas to himself but he was still thinking about his meeting with Todd. He didn't know why he had spoken out. It was as if he were speaking in a dream. It was very careless. But now that he'd said it, he had better be right.

Twenty minutes after Joe arrived at work, everybody seemed to know about what Joe had said about coffee. Joe, of course, had acted upon his own advice right away and had bought a large number of shares in coffee. Others soon followed.

"Hey, what do you know that we don't, Joe?" somebody asked.

"You'd better be right, Faust," said another. "I've just spent all I've got on coffee!"

Everybody bought coffee. Demand forced the price up and up.

"You were right, Joe," somebody told him. "Coffee prices are at an all-time high!"

Prices continued to rise the next day. And the next.

It was now two days after Joe's prediction. It was early in the working day, and all the traders were excited.

"Watch the Faust kid," the other traders said. "When he sells, we sell!"

All eyes were on Joe now. There was nothing he could do about it. What if he was wrong? What if prices went down too soon and traders held on to coffee for too long all because of him? They could lose a great deal of money. But Joe knew in his heart that he wasn't wrong. He smiled with confidence.

"Prices are still rising on coffee!" a trader called out. "Joe Faust said two days and they'd fall. It's nearly that and they're still rising!"

The trader was right. Joe knew coffee prices couldn't keep rising. He sold all his coffee shares right away. With a click of his keyboard they were sold. Joe had made a huge profit. "Sold!" he shouted for all to hear.

Some traders cheered Joe's success. Most made a rush to sell before prices sank. Some were too late and took losses but many made big profits, though few made as much profit as Joe.

It had all gone exactly as Joe had predicted. He was quickly becoming known as a skillful young trader, and it felt good. Very good.

◇◇◇

Brad Benson looked at Joe from behind his office desk.

"Well, Joe, you did it again!" he said.

"Did what, Brad?"

"You know exactly what I'm talking about. Don't pretend you don't!" Brad told him. "But relax. You did well, kid. We made more on coffee than we've ever done. Mind you, the coffee market is now at an all-time low. It doesn't know what hit it. And, to tell the truth, neither do I. Where did you get your information from, Joe? What did you know that we didn't?"

"I just seem to have a natural awareness of the market, Brad," Joe answered. "It's a feeling I get."

"A feeling you get?" Brad said in a raised voice. "Joe, we are not supposed to act on 'feelings we get'! We study the market and use our experience. We're not here to spend large amounts of our clients' money based on our feelings!"

"I was right though, Brad, wasn't I?" said Joe.

"What you did was to start a sales rush based on nothing more than your feelings!" Brad told him. "You're making quite a name for yourself these days, Joe. People are starting to believe what you say. But is what you say based on facts? Or just your 'feelings'? Some might even say that wasn't an honest thing to do, Joe. Some might say you were trying to influence the market by spreading false ideas."

"And what do you say, Brad?" Joe asked.

"I say we're in the business of making a profit, and you made us a profit. A big one. Nice work, kid."

Joe smiled and turned to go.

"Oh, and Joe . . . ," Brad called out.

"Yes, Brad?"

"Don't make it so obvious next time!"

Chapter 4

Private information

Joe could hardly wait for Bonnie to come back from her business trip. He wanted to tell her all about his successes face-to-face. But she wouldn't be back for another few weeks.

Joe was very happy with his success so far. But this, he was sure, was only the beginning. He was right. One week later, as Joe looked at the shares on his computer screen, he saw that the price of shares for tin was low. He just knew that it was the right time to buy shares in the metal.

He didn't tell anybody else this time, though he knew all eyes were on him. This success would be entirely his own.

"Hey, Joe, any more tips?" somebody shouted out.

"You're the expert, Joe. What's the next winner?" asked somebody else.

"Hey, I was just lucky with the coffee!" Joe told them, but few believed him.

Joe knew Brad Benson was watching him. So was everybody else, but Joe wasn't giving anything away. Not yet. First he bought as many tin shares as he could.

Joe couldn't really explain why he felt like this about the shares. It was just a feeling he had, but he trusted that feeling. What Joe didn't know was that a secret deal to open several large canning factories had been reached. Cans for keeping every kind of food from tuna to peaches were made using tin. Brad Benson knew all about it, but Joe didn't. Once the market heard about the deal, tin prices would rise fast.

"Hey, look!" somebody shouted. And there it was—news of the canning factories had reached their screens.

"You'd better hurry, Joe," somebody told him. "Tin prices are going up and up. You don't want to miss this one!"

"Thanks for the tip," Joe said. He didn't say that he had already spent everything he could on tin shares. He was just waiting to sell.

Joe didn't have to wait long. An hour later Joe had a feeling that it was all too good to be true. He knew he had to sell his tin shares right away. Now. At once.

So he did.

"Why are you selling, Joe?" somebody asked. "Do you know something we don't?"

"Just a feeling I had, that's all," Joe told them. "Don't mind me."

"But you could double your profits the way things are going, Joe, if you hang on to those shares," one trader told him.

"Oh, no!" somebody called out. "Look! The canning factory deal has fallen through! No more tin sales! Sell! Sell!"

Tin prices now dropped quickly. Most traders didn't sell in time and lost out. But there always had to be some losers and, just so long as he wasn't one of them, Joe didn't really care. This time he had made a profit by keeping his business to himself. He had made a huge amount of money on the market by using the gift he knew he had and it felt good.

Joe's profits were big, the biggest so far. The only other person to make a large profit was Brad Benson.

Just over a week later, Joe was called in to Brad Benson's office.

"I notice," Brad told Joe, "that you've kept to safe investments for the last week or so. Haven't you had any more 'feelings' about profitable shares recently, Joe? Like the ones you had about coffee? Or how about tin?"

"I noticed you did pretty well with tin shares yourself, Brad," Joe replied. "Did you have a 'feeling' about them, too?"

At first Brad looked annoyed, then he laughed.

"No, Joe, I had information. Private information. You can't rely on feelings all the time. It helps to have something a little more specific."

"So you knew about the canning factories?" Joe asked. "You knew that the deal would fall through?"

"Let's just say that certain of our most valued clients knew," Brad told him. "And they wanted us to use that knowledge to protect their interests. That means our interests, too. But I'm sure I don't have to tell you that, Joe. After all, those 'feelings' you keep having tell me you're playing the same game, right?"

Joe knew that Brad, in admitting to using insider knowledge about shares, was guessing that he did, too. Using insider knowledge in trading was illegal. A city trader who used secret insider knowledge about the market to gain an advantage over other traders could go to jail—if he were caught. Even so, it did happen and they both knew it.

"Well, my 'feelings' are encouraged by a certain source, yes," said Joe. He didn't say that his encouraging source was Rey Todd. Joe knew that if Brad thought they were both using illegal insider knowledge, it could make Brad careless. Who knows what secrets he might give away that were to Joe's advantage? If Joe ever did use insider knowledge, he knew he would be a lot more careful than Brad Benson. Joe smiled as he considered this and Brad saw it.

"I thought so," said Brad, smiling back. "Well, important people are talking about you, Joe. You've certainly been noticed."

"Enough to give me the Investem Life Insurance account, Brad?"

"Now wait a minute!" Brad laughed. "I said you've been noticed, but don't think you can take the place of Dawson Coles just yet. No, be happy with the money you've made—and that's plenty. You'll be promoted soon enough. Just give it time, Joe, give it time."

As Joe went back to his office he knew that he didn't want to wait any longer. He wanted the promotion before he saw Bonnie again. He had to have it! He had Rey Todd's card and he thought about his promise to see him. The time had come.

It was time to make a "special deal" with Todd.

Chapter 5

Rey Todd

Room 113 was farther down in the building than Joe expected. Usually the top people in a company had the offices on the top floor. Not Todd. He sure was a strange little guy.

Todd's office door was made of heavy, dark wood and on the front of it in shiny, gold letters was written Mr. Rey Todd.

That was all.

Joe felt nervous. He was in his new light gray Italian suit. His expensive designer watch told him it was almost three o'clock. He had not made an appointment, but had just rushed home, changed, and come straight here. It just felt like the right thing to do with a man like Todd. But still, now, standing in front of the heavy door, Joe felt nervous. He knew his whole future could depend on this interview.

Joe once more straightened his silk tie and knocked. The door opened. Joe walked in. The room was warmer than he was used to, like a hot kitchen, and there, seated in a green leather armchair, was Todd. He was smoking a cigar and was dressed in his pale suit. Beneath the strong smell of the cigar, Joe could still detect the familiar perfume of Todd's bittersweet cologne.

"Welcome, Joe," said Todd. "I was expecting you. Please, come in."

Joe wondered how Todd knew he was coming, but he wasn't surprised. Todd somehow seemed to know everything.

Joe walked in and the door shut itself behind him with a heavy sound. Joe's shoulders gave a little jump as he heard it.

"Please excuse the door," said Todd. "I like to control it from here. Come on, Joe, sit down next to me."

Joe sat in another green chair. He looked around the room and saw that it was surprisingly small and full of dark wood and old books. There were photographs of successful businessmen on the wall, including one of a smiling Don Smitty. Next to the chairs was a small desk with some old-looking documents on it. Next to the documents was a little knife. It looked extremely sharp. Joe didn't feel comfortable, even though the green chair was soft. He could feel sweat forming already down his backbone as he breathed the thick, warm air. He coughed.

"Does the cigar bother you, Joe?" Todd asked. "I'm sorry— I'm too used to them. I hardly notice the smoke anymore." Todd put out his cigar, but the smell just seemed worse. Joe said nothing, and Todd laughed softly.

"Well, Joe," Todd said. "Why don't you tell me how you've been doing in the past month?"

"Pretty well, sir."

"I'd say more than pretty well, Joe," said Todd with a smile, "judging by your expensive clothes and your fancy sports car. Yes, I'd say you were doing more than pretty well. I'd say you were doing very well, wouldn't you? Sure you would. So, tell me, Joe, why do you think you've had all this success? Do tell me; I'd like to know."

Joe could feel his sweat beneath the silk of his shirt. The smoke was bothering him. The room felt small. Todd, it seemed, was keeping an eye on his progress, and it made him nervous.

"Well, sir," Joe began, "I think I've always had a 'feel' for the market. I just seem to know how things are going almost without thinking about it. And ever since we spoke I remembered your advice about trusting my feelings. It gave me even more confidence and it's sure helped me since then."

"I'm glad you think so, Joe," said Todd. "The gift of good advice can sometimes be very valuable. I call it my gift to promising young individuals whom I notice from time to time. And you're very promising, Joe. Special, even. It was my gift to you, Joe, and I'm so glad it was worth it. In fact, at this very moment, you are being spoken of most highly by the top people in the company. Yes, we think you are just the man to take charge of some of the company's major clients. And you know what that means, Joe?"

Joe nodded. It meant a big promotion. But, most of all, it meant money. Lots and lots of money. The thought of the riches he might achieve made Joe's heart beat faster. And, with them, power.

"With your abilities and, of course, the gift of my advice, you could have all the money you ever dreamed of. You said you would give anything for that, didn't you, Joe?"

"I guess I did," Joe said softly.

"Well, now you have your big chance, Joe. I'm going to put to you an offer that will make you seriously rich if you take it. But if you don't take it, I'm telling you now, I'll see to it that you never get beyond being a small-time trader for us or for anybody else." Todd looked Joe straight in the eye. "How do you feel about that, Joe?"

Joe felt as if all his dreams had come true. He knew that Todd could do exactly what he said. But Joe wasn't worried about turning anything down. Joe loved making money. He loved spending it, too. Most of all, he loved the power of controlling money. Now he wanted to control huge sums of money. That was where the real power was. That was what he would do anything for. The thought of losing the chance to have this power was just not an option for him. Not at all. No, sir.

"I want to work for the company, sir," Joe said with feeling. "Yes, I meant what I said: I'll do anything for this job. Whatever you say, I'll do it. What do I have to do, sir?"

"Well now, Joe," said Todd, "that's easy. I'm offering you a contract for life with the company, Joe. Why, just think of the possibilities of spending your entire life making money for the company—and, of course, becoming an extremely wealthy man yourself. In return we expect you to be with us, heart and soul, in making profit. Your total commitment is absolutely required and will, of course, be permanent."

Joe wanted this more than anything. A life contract at last! Life contracts were unusual but not unheard of—he'd heard that Smitty had one.

"What do I have to do, sir?" Joe asked.

"Just sign a contract," said Todd. "Oh, there're lots of words in it, but it all comes down to what I said: make profits for us and nobody else. No free work to help the planet or to support a charity or any of that kind of nonsense—unless it makes a profit in some way, of course. But if you break your contract in any way, we'll be after you for every cent you ever made. We'll bring you down, boy. You'll never work again, for us or for anybody else. OK?"

Joe looked at the contract. The paper was thicker than usual, like fine leather, and a dark yellow color. The writing was small but he had seen this kind of thing before. It was full of things requiring you to work for them and nobody else. But he knew that people could get out of this kind of contract if they really wanted to. You just needed a good lawyer. Nobody expects to work for anybody forever. Not these days. He didn't think he needed to read any more of it.

"I'll sign," said Joe. "Where do I put my name?"

Todd picked up one of the documents from his desk.

"I have it all right here," Todd said. "Don't worry; it's all quite plain and simple. Just hold out your hand first, please."

Joe wondered what this was about. He held out his hand, and Todd produced a small pot and an old-looking pen. Then he picked up the little sharp knife.

"Hey!" Joe called out. "What are you doing with that?"

"Now don't be nervous, Joe," Todd said. "We're a very old company and we like to take a traditional approach to these matters. It's just an old custom of ours. We always sign important contracts in blood. Lots of companies have their old customs—this is ours. Now, hold out your hand, please."

Joe hesitated. Some companies did have strange customs, it was true. And this was an old company. He held out his hand.

"This won't hurt a bit," Todd said. It didn't. Todd just touched Joe's thumb with the point of the knife. A few drops of Joe's blood fell into the pot. Todd put the pen into the pot, and then held it out to Joe.

"Just sign on the line here, Joe," Todd said, though his voice sounded strangely excited beneath its usual cheerful manner.

Just for a moment, Joe thought Todd's round face looked different. Now he didn't look like a friendly uncle at all. Todd licked his thin lips hungrily as he watched Joe's hand reach out for the pen. Joe noticed yellow teeth beneath the thin lips.

Just for a moment, Joe felt a wave of fear, even terror, and turned his head away. For that brief moment, all he wanted to do was scream "NO!" and run away as fast as he could. But the moment passed. He told himself not to be like a frightened kid. All he had to do was sign, and money and success would be his. After all, that's what he had always wanted.

And indeed, when he looked again, Todd's face was as round and friendly as ever. Joe told himself he had nothing to fear at all. Nothing. Todd smiled and Joe felt relaxed again. He took the pen. He signed. He put the pen down.

"Excellent!" cried Todd cheerfully. "That's it. Now that wasn't so bad, was it?"

"No, Mr. Todd," said Joe. He was feeling a little silly already about his moment of fear. He felt a lot better now about his new future. As Joe left room 113 the door shut loudly behind him. Alone in the elevator going back to his own floor, he thought of the deal he had made.

That, he said to himself, wasn't bad at all. No, sir.

Chapter 6

The Investem Life Insurance account

The next day, as Joe was busy working at his computer, he looked up and saw that Brad Benson was walking straight toward him.

Brad took Joe's hand and shook it warmly.

"You've got the Investem Life Insurance account, Joe! You start tomorrow!" Brad looked pleased. "Somebody really important must like you!"

"But what about Dawson Coles?" Joe asked in surprise. "I thought he handled that?"

"Not anymore," said Brad. "One of the top Investem Life Insurance people asked for you personally. They said you'd been highly recommended, so Coles has been given another client. I don't suppose he liked that one bit. But it's good news for you, Joe. Enjoy!"

"Thanks!" Joe said

"You won't thank me if you make a bad job of it," Brad said, not unkindly. "This is the big one, Joe. Good luck, but be careful, OK?"

Joe was happy; he had his dream promotion at last and now was his chance to make some serious money. When he got back to his apartment, he looked at his personal e-mails. He was happy to see that there was one from Bonnie.

Hi Joe

I've had a good time here in Toronto learning all about business law (ho-hum!) and I'm always amazed at the things some people get up to! But I said I'm not going to talk about work and I'm not going to. I'm just looking forward to seeing you again and listening to some jazz with you at Macey's Bar. That will be soon, darling, because I'm coming home early—next Saturday!

I don't expect you've become a millionaire just yet, but I do I expect a whole weekend doing fun things that have nothing to do with work and everything to do with you.

See you at your place—can't wait!

Your Bonnie

X X X

After reading the e-mail Joe was even happier. He went to bed early to be ready for his new job the next morning. But first he had to read a few files about insurance.

Three hours went by before he got to bed.

Investem Life Insurance was very big indeed. It was one of the biggest clients Joe's company had. Insurance relied on good investments to make good profits, and it was now Joe's job to make those investments for them. The amount of money Joe now had responsibility for was enough to take his breath away. Just one mistake on Joe's part could lose the Insurance company—and Joe's own company—many, many millions of dollars!

Joe had gotten what he wanted: the "big one," as he called it. He felt nervous but excited. His luck with shares had all seemed to come together at the right time—ever since seeing Rey Todd. That was good timing, Joe thought.

◇◇◇

Joe looked around his new private office on the twentieth floor. It had once belonged to Don Smitty, though Dawson Coles had, for some reason, refused to work there. Not that Joe cared. Dawson Coles could go to hell. The office had a fine view of Manhattan from the window. It was very comfortable, too, with leather chairs and expensive furniture. Even the computers were placed on fine tables. But all the computer screens were there for work, so Joe got to work right away.

Joe sat down and looked at the market on his main computer screen. He began to buy. At first he chose all of the "safe" investments he could, always a good idea with insurance companies. But, so far, there was nothing that made him think "Yes, this is the one!"

Joe knew his feeling for profit had worked for him in the past. Would his feelings work for him now? Was Rey Todd right about that "gift" he mentioned?

Then Joe noticed something in the pattern of one of the investments that suddenly hit him. It was as if a light had been turned on in his brain.

"Copper!" he shouted.

Somehow Joe just knew that the price of that particular metal would go down over the next hour, just as he knew it would go up soon after. He knew that prices didn't have to go up very much when you bought millions of shares. Huge profits could be made, even with a small increase, if you sold them before they went down again.

Joe knew that even he wouldn't have dreamed of doing this a few weeks before. Not with these sums of money. Smitty, he now knew, had lost millions when he put everything into one investment. He lost everything all right. Now he's dead, thought Joe. But I'm not Smitty, Joe told himself, and I have a real feeling for profit. It's my gift, just as Todd said!

Brad Benson came in to check on Joe's progress.

"Joe!" he cried out when he saw the computer screen. "Why are you investing in copper? It's been going down, and there's no reason for it to go up again as far as I can see. Look, it's your first day in the job, and I'm only saying this for your own good, Joe. Be careful!"

Joe turned and looked at Benson. "Brad?"

"Yeah, Joe?"

"Just leave me alone to get on with my job, OK?"

Brad Benson shook his head and left.

Joe waited for thirty-five minutes, staring hard at the copper prices as they went down and down. His suit was dark with sweat and his silk tie now lay on the floor.

Then it reached the point where copper prices stopped going down. Quickly, Joe bought all that he could and waited. Copper prices rose by just a few points. Then a few more.

Joe had bought millions of them. Even now he could make a big profit if he sold them. Instead, he waited. His hand was held above his computer keyboard shaking with nerves as he waited to sell everything for the highest possible price. But the shares continued to rise and rise. Finally, they stopped.

"Now!"

With one quick click of a key Joe made millions of dollars. He sat back in his chair with relief. His feeling for profit had not let him down. Now he felt it never would; he felt like he was on top of the world.

He looked at the computer screen. Copper prices had already begun to sink.

Boy! That was something! Joe thought. He had enjoyed making all that money, not only for the money he earned himself, though that was very much appreciated. No, he especially enjoyed controlling huge amounts of money. It was a good feeling. Very good.

Joe knew he was now a rich man—his bonus alone from this would be millions of dollars. But this was only just the beginning. For he wanted more. Much more.

And nothing and nobody were going to stop him.

Chapter 7

Rich and richer

Bonnie's eyes opened wide as she stared at the expensive silver-colored convertible sports car. They had just gotten out of the terminal at New York's LaGuardia Airport, and all her bags were on the ground next to the car.

"You mean this is yours, Joe?" Bonnie asked, hardly able to believe that Joe could own such a costly possession.

"She sure is," Joe answered, proudly. "And this is yours!" Joe handed Bonnie a small box, and when she opened it she found a gold ring. On the ring was the biggest, reddest ruby she had ever seen. Bonnie, for once, was speechless as she sat down in the car and stared at the bright red jewel. "Don't ask how much it was," Joe told her. "It wasn't cheap!" But Bonnie knew that it must have been worth at least a hundred thousand dollars and maybe a lot more. Joe knew he had, at last, impressed her. He started up the engine.

"This is better than a yellow New York cab any day, huh? Now, shall we go . . . ?"

"You've had a big smile all over your face ever since we left LaGuardia Airport and now we're driving into Riverside," Bonnie said as the wind blew her hair. "Aren't you going to tell me what's been going on?"

"Don't you like Riverside?" asked Joe, laughing as he said it.

"Sure I do," Bonnie answered. "But it's one of the most expensive places to live in the city and you don't live here!"

Joe stopped the car outside a smart-looking apartment block. "I don't live here now, but I will in a couple of days. See that apartment on the top floor there? The one with the big windows? That's my new address!"

"It's beautiful," said Bonnie. "But all this money, Joe . . . I don't understand. You'd need to be really rich to afford all this."

Joe smiled and then laughed again. "You told me not to say anything about work until I made my first million dollars," he said. "Well, now I can because I have. In fact, I've made much more than a million, honey! And I'm handling the Investem Life Insurance account! I'm rich and I'm going to get richer every day!"

"It's all happened so quickly, Joe," said Bonnie. "How on earth did you do it?"

Joe saw the look in Bonnie's eyes. They were wide with admiration and he liked that. They also looked a little confused and he wasn't sure if that meant she doubted him. He didn't like that.

Joe wanted so much for Bonnie to think he had done everything by himself. Then he thought of Rey Todd and the contract he signed. He didn't want to tell Bonnie about that, about the blood, the knife, and Todd's hungry look when he signed. No, she wouldn't understand. Not yet.

"I just have a feel for this kind of thing," Joe told her in a joking way. "Business and stuff. You know how we young brilliant types are once we get going. You want the details . . . ?"

"There's no time to talk about work right now, Joe Faust," Bonnie laughed. "You're going to take me home so I can change into something sexy."

"And then . . . ?" asked Joe, raising his eyes.

"And then we go to the best restaurant in town—and you're paying!"

◇◇◇

Joe's skill at making profits didn't let him down. The market had never seen a success story like his before. Over the next few months the headlines in the business papers were all about him:

Faust Success for Investem Insurance Company

Joe Faust Businessman of the Year

Faust Tops Earnings Table

They were all full of stories about the new "wonder-boy of Manhattan." Joe loved it. He was now one of the richest individuals in the city. He was also one of the hardest-working traders the company had ever known. The profits he made for them were amazing, and his personal wealth was now almost beyond counting. He was more than a millionaire—he was a billionaire.

Bonnie worked hard, too, and she loved her job. Because they both spent long times apart, Joe tried to make their times together special. At first he and Bonnie both enjoyed buying clothes, going to restaurants, and having expensive weekend holidays. It was during dinner at their favorite Italian restaurant that Joe first asked Bonnie to marry him. "You won't have to work anymore—not with all the money I make!" he told her.

Bonnie laughed. "Oh, yeah? And what do I do—stay at home and keep your dinner warm while you work late? I don't think so!"

Joe hadn't expected this reaction. Bonnie never talked about work. Joe thought she would be only too glad to leave it all for him. "But I make all the money we need," he said. "You won't need to work."

"Look, Joe, if you have so much money already, then why don't you stop working and quit your job?" asked Bonnie.

"If you quit your job, I'll quit mine. We'll both live happily ever after. What do you say?"

"I couldn't do that, Bonnie," Joe said. "I love my work and you know it."

"I know, Joe," Bonnie said quietly. "I love my job, too. Look, Joe, I love you, but let's think about marrying each other when we're not both married to our jobs. For now, why don't we just enjoy being together when we can?"

"OK, Bonnie," Joe said, then had an idea. "Hey, what if I took some time off? I mean, I could work fewer hours, or even take a vacation for a couple of months? The company must know how hard I've been working for them. They owe me some time."

"That's a good idea, Joe," Bonnie answered. "But my company is still keeping me busy. I can't just drop cases to take time off when I want to. But there's no reason why you shouldn't relax a little more. Do you think you can do that? It'll do you good."

Joe felt disappointed that Bonnie wouldn't take time off too, but he didn't say so. "I guess so," he said with a smile. "After all, what's the use of making money if you don't enjoy it?"

The following week, Bonnie was away working on a big case—again. This time she was going to be away for almost two months.

The company owed Joe some vacation time and he decided to take two months off. At first it felt strange not to be on his daily hunt for profit. But hadn't he earned it? He was sure nearly everybody he knew in the company would agree, wouldn't they? Why shouldn't he enjoy a good, long vacation? And if Bonnie wasn't there, well, he would have to enjoy his vacation without her.

Joe wanted to show New York that he could play as hard as he worked. He set about this with all his usual energy. He wanted to show everybody his new wealth. He wanted Bonnie to hear about him having a good time of it, to realize he could enjoy life without work for a while. Why couldn't she do the same? Why couldn't she? He planned three big parties over the next two months and invited many famous and fashionable people to each of them.

The first party was the smallest with only two hundred people. It was held in his new apartment and went on nearly all night. He missed Bonnie, but by the end of the evening he was in the arms of a young actress. She told him he was much better looking than her leading men. After a few drinks Joe thought she looked like Bonnie and, after a few more, he behaved as if she was. In the morning he lay alone in his bed; his head was hurting and the actress was gone. Joe couldn't remember much about her; all he saw was an empty space next to him where Bonnie should be.

The second party was bigger. Joe hired rooms in a big hotel and had the latest rock band play for his five hundred guests. The guests were mostly famous people from show business and sports. Joe kept a clear head that evening, although some of his guests didn't follow his example. One well-known footballer even went up to him and asked, "Who is this Faust guy, anyway??" But all the society magazines knew.

The next day's newspapers were full of stories from guests who had been there and even some who had not. Joe read about people he hardly knew who were claiming he was "a great guy" and "a good friend of mine." Some were saying that he had invited them because he had supported their favorite charity or political party, or used a product they made. None of it was true. But Joe said nothing. He was getting an idea of what it was like to be famous and rich.

People pretended to like him when all they wanted was his money or his influence. Well, he couldn't blame them for that, but he didn't like it.

Joe missed his work, too. Even though he had taken time off as he had promised Bonnie he would, he found he kept thinking about new investments and promising markets. He missed the business of making profits. It was like a great hunger to him, which he needed to satisfy.

But first there was party number three. This was going to be the biggest with one thousand guests. It would take over a whole floor of one of Manhattan's best hotels, and many important rich people would be there, including people from the world of business. A top jazz band was providing the music. The party was going to be huge.

This time Bonnie would be there, too. She had e-mailed him to say she would arrive at the party halfway through. Joe would make sure all his careful preparations worked out exactly as planned: he would be the center of attention; famous people would say what a great guy he was; and businesspeople would want to be seen with him. He, his wealth, and his success would be there for the world to admire.

Bonnie would see it all.

And this time, he told himself, it's going to be perfect.

Chapter 8

A party in Manhattan

The Manhattan streets were busy on the night of Joe's third and biggest party. It was raining heavily, but even the rain couldn't stop photographers taking their pictures for the next day's newspapers. Stars from TV, the movies, and the world of high finance stepped out from their luxury cars. They hurried down a wet, red carpet that led them to the bright lights of the hotel entrance. Fans and curious people in the street cheered and waved. Some famous guests stayed for a while to talk to newspaper and TV reporters or to shake welcoming hands as attendants held expensive umbrellas over them. They had to talk to their admirers, even in rain like this.

"Yes, Joe Faust is a good friend of mine," an aging film director told one reporter as TV cameras looked on. He had met Joe once for a few seconds during a film opening.

"And do you think he'll be putting his money into your next film?" the reporter asked.

"*Giant Monkeys from Mars III?*" the director winked. "Well, let's just say we both know a good investment when we see one."

By ten o'clock in the evening the party was well underway. Joe was dressed in a white dinner suit with a black tie. His fingers wore gold rings with costly jewels shining from them. His wristwatch, too, was rich with jewels. He believed he looked good and he considered himself to be much admired. He had become even more admirable, it

49

seemed to him, as his wealth had increased. Many famous people now claimed him as their close friend. Some of these people acted as if they were doing him a favor by advising him to invest in their businesses. Once you're rich, Joe thought, it's amazing how friendly people can be.

"You know," one older businessman had said during the evening as he put his arm around Joe's shoulder, "I'm telling you this first because I like you, but there's money to be made in fish farming."

Shortly afterwards, a television producer told him confidentially, "I'm giving you this chance, Joe, to be a major investor in my new TV show about teenage superheroes. I'm telling you, Joe, it's going to be big!"

Others sought his company just to be seen with him, while some, wishing to seem less obvious, ignored him, hoping he would recognize their famous faces as they "just happened" to be close by. Joe didn't like it when people pretended not to recognize him; they weren't there for that, so he made sure he ignored them instead.

At first Joe had enjoyed all the attention. His parties had allowed him to show off his wealth, this party most of all. Now he was starting to feel differently. Now all these new "friends" were drinking champagne that cost a thousand dollars a bottle as if it were water. They were eating expensive food as if they expected it every day. Maybe they did, Joe thought. Most of these people have never been poor, they've always had everything. Why should they be impressed by wealth?

Joe was beginning to dislike what he saw. But would he be like them if he was in their position? Probably, though the thought didn't please him.

He looked around. Some asked him for business advice, others tried to give it. Yet behind the smiles he saw jealousy and in the admiring comments he sensed envy. His dislike was turning to disgust. Is this what my success has gotten me? he thought.

Joe now knew that to these people his personality and good looks didn't matter. The only thing that mattered was that they believed in his amazing ability to make money. And that, he realized with a shock, was all that mattered to him, too.

City traders like himself appreciated his abilities. Not that Joe liked them, particularly, but he knew their admiring comments were genuine. Only they could understand what he had done, even if they were often jealous. Joe also knew that if he ever stopped being at the top, most of them would be only too happy to walk all over him.

During a quieter moment, Joe shut his eyes and listened to the jazz band. He was beginning to think that maybe he would rather be alone at Macey's Bar than here with these people when his thoughts turned to Todd. Joe hadn't invited Todd; the idea had never occurred to him. Now Todd's round face kept disturbing his thoughts. It made him feel uneasy. Joe realized what a fool he'd been. Todd must know about him taking two whole months off. He felt Todd would surely disapprove and think he should be working for more profits instead of giving big parties. That's what Todd would think. What disturbed Joe most of all was the cold realization that he, too, now felt the same way. He would rather be finding ways of making fat profits from trading in the city than be standing here.

When Joe opened his eyes, Todd was standing across the room in his pale suit staring at him. What was he doing here? Joe felt his mouth go dry. A cold sweat dripped down his back. He shut his eyes once more, then opened them again.

Todd was gone.

Then Joe saw Bonnie coming towards him. She had a red dress on and wore diamonds around her neck. She looked beautiful. And she was holding on to the arm of a smiling Dawson Coles. What was she doing with him? She was his girl!

"Joe!" Bonnie cried out happily. "What a party! And look who's been showing me around while you've been the center of attention."

Dawson Coles was at least ten years older than Joe. He was dressed in a stylish black evening suit and looked very relaxed and happy. He shook Joe by the hand. "I appreciate the invitation, Joe. You know, I'd say they got the right man for the Investem Life Insurance job," he said. "I was mad as hell at first but I know when I'm beaten. Joe, you're the best at this game, and I wish you all the luck in the world."

"Why that's kind of you to say so, Dawson," Joe answered. Joe was puzzled at first. Was Dawson actually being nice to him? Why?

Bonnie looked excited and said, "Dawson has told me about his plans for the future, Joe, and I think you'll be interested. Tell Joe, Dawson!"

"Well," Dawson looked down. "The fact is, Joe, I'm retiring from the company. I've done pretty well for myself . . ."

"Dawson means he's loaded with money!" put in Bonnie cheerfully.

". . . and I'm going to make some private investments in some worthy concerns," Dawson said smiling.

"What Dawson means," Bonnie said happily, "is he's going to invest in things that will help the planet instead of bleeding it dry!"

"Bonnie has a colorful way of expressing things," Dawson said. "But, as always, she has understood my meaning correctly."

Joe's eyes opened wide in spite of himself. "Dawson, I had no idea—I wish you luck. But what about the company? What does the company say?"

"The company?" Dawson answered. "The company has had enough out of me. Now the company—with all due respect—can go to hell."

Joe didn't know if he should admire Dawson Coles or not. Part of him jumped for joy at hearing his words, while another part of him disapproved of Dawson Coles for turning away from the all-important business of making profits.

"I really don't know what to say, Dawson," Joe replied.

"Then don't say anything for now, Joe," Dawson told him. "I've mentioned a few ideas to Bonnie. Maybe we can discuss them over dinner soon?"

Ideas? Joe thought to himself. Has Bonnie been talking over some ideas with Dawson Coles that concern me? Why didn't she ask me first?

"Why, yes," Joe answered carefully. "I'd be very interested."

"Good," said Dawson. "I'll be in touch." And he left to speak to some other guests. Bonnie looked up at Joe and smiled.

"Don't you see, Joe?" she said. "It's not impossible! Dawson has made all the money he needs; now he's going to use it to help people! You're a billionaire now, Joe, so why don't we do the same? We can get married and you could get out of this business! I'd take care of all the legal side of things, and we'd make a great team! Don't you see, Joe—everybody wins! What do you say?"

Joe's eyes opened wide in horror. The idea of not using his money to make profits was unthinkable to him now. It was ridiculous.

He looked at Bonnie's smiling face. In it he saw the beautiful girl he loved but now he also saw the silly face of a young woman who had no idea of what he was involved with. She didn't know about Todd and she didn't understand about his own increasing passion for profit. Making money was his business; nothing else mattered. Surely she could see that? Couldn't she?

Yet he knew that he loved her and she loved him. In the end he said, "I don't want to talk about it here, Bonnie. Let's save it for later and just enjoy the party for now."

"I guess you're right," answered Bonnie, who held Joe's hand tightly and added, "but it's great what Dawson has done, Joe. It'll be great for us, too. Just wait and see!"

Across the room a young woman was looking at them. It was the actress Joe had met at his first party. Joe had not noticed her all evening, and she hadn't liked that.

Not one bit.

Chapter 9

Headlines

Joe sat in the café of the hotel. The party the night before had finished well past midnight and had been a great success. He was having a late morning coffee while he waited for Bonnie to join him. He closed his eyes and listened to some jazz on his personal music player while he waited. He felt a tap on his shoulder. He smiled.

"You're late again!" he laughed. He switched off his music, turned around, and opened his eyes, expecting to see Bonnie. But it wasn't Bonnie.

It was Todd.

The smell of Todd's bittersweet cologne was already mixing with the smell of Joe's coffee. Joe's mouth was open in speechless surprise.

"Yes, Joe," said Todd softly, as he pulled up a chair. "I am late, though not too late, I think."

Joe's heart felt as if it was suddenly beating twice as fast. If Todd had shouted out loud he could not have made Joe feel more alarmed. Joe wanted to speak, but Todd spoke first, his voice almost a whisper.

"I've been seeing your name in the newspapers, Joe," he said in quiet anger. "Now, normally, I like to see your name in the papers. I like to see it in the business papers, Joe, with your name behind a profitable deal. That's what I like. That's what the company likes. That's what we agreed on, Joe. But what do I see? I see Joe Faust's name next to big parties with famous people who all want a piece of you. I keep on seeing it. Now why is that, Joe?"

"I've just had some time off, a little holiday," Joe said. "What's wrong with that?"

"Two weeks is a holiday," Todd replied, his angry voice no longer quiet. "Two months is a denial of your responsibilities to the company, Joe. It's a betrayal of your duty to profit."

"Haven't I made you enough profit while I've been here?" Joe asked, his voice containing both alarm and anger.

"We can never, ever have too much profit, Joe," Todd answered. "I think you know that; you've always known that. You see, Joe, you and I are really very alike. We know what we want. We know what we're good at. Nothing else satisfies us. If I'm wrong, please tell me."

Joe couldn't. The excitement, the thrill of working in the market was everything to him, and even now he was anxious to get back to it. As for being like Todd, the thought made Joe's blood run cold. Joe looked at Todd with his round face and almost permanent smile. Beneath that smile was an unlimited hunger for gain that denied all else—all life, all joy. I'm not like him! Joe told himself. No, I couldn't be like that! He thought, but in his heart he knew it wasn't true. Didn't his reaction to Bonnie's suggestion tell him that?

"Good," Todd said, as if he read what was going on in Joe's mind. "Now I expect you know by now about Dawson Coles leaving the company? Unlike you, we chose not to offer him one of our life-term contracts. He had promise, yes, but not like you, Joe, oh no. He has plans of his own now, which I believe he wishes to share with you and Miss Perez. But that's not going to happen, is it, Joe? After all, you signed a contract with us for life and we take that very seriously indeed."

Joe said nothing but looked down, unable to face Todd. Whatever he did, he now believed that getting out of his contract with Todd was all but impossible for reasons that made him very afraid. After all, it was a life contract. He could sense Todd's eyes looking into his heart. Was Todd seeing how much like him Joe was becoming? Joe realized with horror that he was.

"I knew we had an understanding," said Todd. "You and I belong to the company, Joe. We always will." Todd got up and walked away.

Joe couldn't look as Todd left. Was he really like Todd? The thought made him feel sick inside. He sat without moving as his coffee went cold and the smell of cologne faded away.

"Hi, Joe!"

It was Bonnie. She was dressed in sky blue and smelled of fresh flowers. She pulled up a chair, the one Todd had sat in. "Hey, you look terrible. Are you OK?"

The sight of Bonnie's smiling face after seeing Todd was a relief to Joe. He felt that she alone knew the real Joe Faust; she of all people would understand. He loved her. He would tell her about the situation he was in. He would tell her everything. It was only right, he thought. So Joe told Bonnie all about Todd and his contract, even about the blood.

Bonnie listened carefully throughout and didn't speak until Joe had finished.

"Well, I'll say one thing," Bonnie began. "Our Mr. Rey Todd knows his psychology. He's scared the hell out of you! Why, he's even got you believing the company owns you for life. But you don't really believe that, do you?"

"Well, a contract has been signed," Joe said quietly.

"You call that a contract?" Bonnie said angrily. "A contract for life signed in your own blood? Can't you see that was all a little show to scare you, Joe? It's true there are some strange customs out there, but this one has no place in business."

"But I signed it, Bonnie," Joe said, "for life."

"Yeah, that's what they always want you to believe. But nobody can sign you up to a company for life, Joe. They don't own you. There's not a court of law in the land that would support a contract like this. You can leave anytime you like, Joe. Unless . . . ,"

Joe looked up. "Unless what, Bonnie?"

". . . unless you want to stay. But now you know what kind of people you're dealing with, that isn't going to be a problem, is it? Is it?"

"If what you say is right, Bonnie, and I can leave any time I like, then what's to stop me making as much money as I want, then leaving when I want to?" Joe answered.

Bonnie looked sad. "Absolutely nothing, Joe. You can do that, that is, if that's what you really want. But you're the richest man in Manhattan now, Joe. Do you want to make even more money? Is that it, Joe? Haven't you got enough yet?"

"Look, Bonnie," Joe said, "It's not just the money. I've got a job I've always wanted. I love the City. Who cares if the contract is a little . . . unusual. I love trading!"

"Is that all you love, Joe?" Bonnie asked. "I thought you loved me, too? Look, you can still trade, Joe. Dawson got himself out; so can you, if you really want to."

"How about a couple more years?" Joe suggested. "Two years, then I leave, then we make our plans. How about that, huh?"

"Joe," Bonnie said quietly, "you should hear yourself! Todd did a deal with you, now you're trying to do a deal with me! You're being just like him! You're trying to treat our future together as if it were some business contract! Is that all I am to you now? Is it? You have to ask yourself, Joe, what's more important to you—a future with me or with Todd? A life with me . . . or with him? That's what it comes down to."

"Hey, Bonnie," Joe said, his voice unable to contain his growing anger, "don't you think you're taking this a little too seriously?"

Bonnie was almost in tears. "I'm taking it very seriously, Joe. But I don't think you're taking it seriously enough. Look, we could work this out together or you could work alone. You need to decide soon, Joe. Let me know when you've made your mind up. I'm going home."

Bonnie got up to leave and Joe, as he watched her go, saw her glance at the day's newspapers as they lay on one of the café tables. She picked one up and read it for a few moments before throwing the paper back onto the table. She walked up to him, slapped him hard across his face, then walked out quickly without looking back.

Joe, his hand on his cheek, was shocked but curious. What had Bonnie read to make her so angry? Joe went to the table and picked up the newspaper. On the front page in big letters it read:

ACTRESS REVEALS SHE IS LOVER OF
MULTIMILLIONAIRE JOE FAUST:
Exclusive interview inside.

Chapter 10

Rise and fall

"Aagh!!"

Joe woke up in the middle of the night again, alarmed, his pillow once more damp with sweat. Todd had been appearing in his dreams more and more, the round face telling him, urging him on to make profits and ever more profits. In this last dream Joe saw his own blood bleeding away from his hand until there was no blood left. It had all disappeared into the dark yellow pages of his contract.

He felt terrified. Bonnie's words came back to him, "You're being just like him!" Just like Todd. The thing that made Joe most afraid was the thought that Bonnie might be right—he might be just like Todd.

◇◇◇

Joe sat in his sports car and looked out the window. It was a pale, cold day. He was parked in the Bronx on the street where he was born. The buildings were old and in a poor state, some left as burnt-out shells by fires from years before. Bitter November winds blew newspapers down the street. People wrapped in coats and scarves looked at him as they passed by. Joe opened his electric window, and cold air rushed in. He thought about what his life had become.

A month ago he had been promoted to Head Investment Advisor. He was now Benson's boss and was personally in charge of huge amounts of the company's money.

Then two weeks ago Bonnie had left him. Not because of the actress with whom he had been stupid for one night with. There was no love affair between them, as the woman had claimed. Bonnie had been angry, but that wasn't why she left him. No, it was because he chose to stay with the company. Bonnie told him they could have no future together. She gave him back her ruby ring. He still had it with him now, in his jacket pocket. He remembered how she had cried.

Just this morning he had seen a picture in the newspaper of Bonnie walking to a public meeting about raising money for the poor. She was arm in arm with Dawson Coles. Joe could tell from her expression that she was more than just a friend. Had she ever really loved him, Joe? How could she do this to him? But it didn't matter anymore. Bonnie was gone.

Joe was unhappy. Fine food and expensive clothes were now just things to eat and things to wear. His rich man's apartment was just a roof over his head. That was why he was here on the street where it had all begun for him. He wanted to remind himself why he had struggled so hard to escape the poor life he had as a child. He had never wanted to be poor again. Not ever!

And now he was rich, richer than he had ever dreamed he could be. He had everything money could buy, he thought. But he couldn't buy everything. He had no family. He lived alone. Joe asked himself why he didn't do what Bonnie had wanted him to do. He could have left the company and married her. They could have worked together to help people. Why didn't he?

Joe knew why. In the end he had gone back to his job for the thrill of controlling money, for the excitement he felt in creating profit and more profit. It wasn't the money that mattered any more. It was the feeling he got when he made a big profit that made him feel happy, even if it was only for a short time. He sought that feeling above everything else, and his desire for that feeling was now stronger than anything else he knew, even his love for Bonnie. But all the money in the world wouldn't be enough to satisfy him, he thought sadly.

Joe looked again down the windblown street. He had hoped that seeing where he came from might put back in him some of his old sense of purpose in life. But it didn't. There was only one thing that still gave him that, only one place that made him feel anything at all these days.

Joe took the ruby ring out of his jacket pocket and threw it out into the street. As he drove back to his office the first snowflakes of evening began to fall.

"Are you sure, boss?" asked Brad Benson. "That's a hell of a lot of the company's money you're risking there."

"If you can't take the risk, leave," Joe said coldly.

Brad shook his head and left.

Joe had put everything he could into shares in new electrical developments. It was the biggest deal he had ever made, and if it fell through even the company might not be able to recover.

Joe needed to feel the thrill of control again, more than ever before. He no longer cared about the company or the money. All he cared about was seeing if he could increase the risks he took to increase profits, to make them greater and to make his control more satisfying. The bigger the risk, the bigger the thrill. It was becoming harder to do, and this was the biggest risk he had ever taken with the company's money. Only a risk like this could give him a chance to experience the excitement of success that was the only thing his life meant to him now.

But would it?

His hands lay over the keyboard waiting for the right moment to sell. It was just like it used to be. Joe waited and waited. Would prices drop or rise? They rose and, when he was sure they would rise no more, he put his finger down on the keyboard and made the company a fortune the like of which even they had never experienced before.

From the other room Joe heard Benson cheer loudly.

Joe knew this was his biggest profit ever. He would be seen as the greatest city trader Manhattan had ever seen. He should be screaming with excitement.

But Joe had felt no thrill, just a tired emptiness. The thrill of making profits was all he had had, and now even that was dead. Now his heart felt that all the life, all the joy in it was gone. It felt like a stone. And all the while, there was the image of Todd in his mind, his soft southern voice urging him to make more profit, profit, profit. Was this all he had left now? Was this all that he could hope for? Was he really the same as Todd?

Joe couldn't stand it anymore.

"To hell with you, Todd!" he screamed. "To hell with you!"

Joe looked at the window. There was one way he could rid himself of that round face and soft southern voice.

Smitty had been right.

◇◇◇

On his way to his interview, a young man with short, blond hair and wearing glasses was reading the top story in the day's newspaper:

Billionaire Trader Jumps to Death after Record Profit

Shaking his head, the young man put the paper into a trash can and straightened his tie. He knocked on the dark wooden door. It opened.

"Welcome, Sam," said Todd in a cheerful voice. "I'm glad to see you. Sit right down."

As Sam Lazlo sat down, he could smell the sickly smell of cigar smoke and bittersweet cologne.

DON SMITTY

JOE FAUST

Review: Chapters 1–4

A. Match the characters in the story with their description.

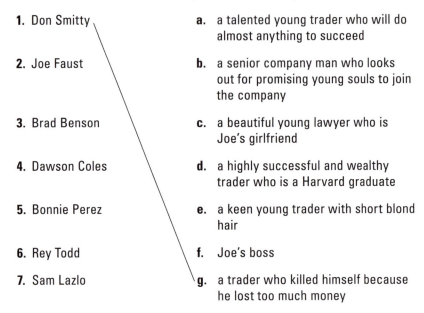

1. Don Smitty

2. Joe Faust

3. Brad Benson

4. Dawson Coles

5. Bonnie Perez

6. Rey Todd

7. Sam Lazlo

a. a talented young trader who will do almost anything to succeed

b. a senior company man who looks out for promising young souls to join the company

c. a beautiful young lawyer who is Joe's girlfriend

d. a highly successful and wealthy trader who is a Harvard graduate

e. a keen young trader with short blond hair

f. Joe's boss

g. a trader who killed himself because he lost too much money

B. Read each statement and circle whether it is true (T) or false (F).

1. Joe used the Internet to buy and sell shares.　　　　T / F

2. Joe didn't mind his girlfriend working for Dawson Coles.　　T / F

3. Joe follows Sam Lazlo's advice about coffee.　　　　T / F

4. Rey Todd seems to know all about Joe.　　　　T / F

5. Joe knows that Brad Benson has been dishonest.　　　T / F

C. Choose the best answer for each question.

1. What three interests do Joe and Bonnie have in common?

a. a love of money

b. sports

c. jazz music

d. good food

e. a love of travel

f. a love of Manhattan

g. fast cars

2. Which statement best describes what Joe thinks of Dawson Coles?

a. He admires him.

b. He thinks Dawson wants to steal his girlfriend.

c. He thinks Dawson's success is due to his money and social connections.

d. He thinks Dawson is a bad businessman.

D. Match each word from chapters 1–4 with its definition.

1. jazz		**a.**	a kind of perfume
2. bonus		**b.**	a person with a high level of knowledge or skill in something
3. cologne		**c.**	a type of modern music that first came from black musicians in the southern USA
4. predict		**d.**	know about something that will happen in the future
5. expert		**e.**	an extra amount of money given as a reward

Review: Chapters 5–7

A. Match each question with the correct answer.

1. What was unusual about Rey Todd's office being on a lower floor?

2. What tells Todd that Joe has been doing more than "pretty well"?

3. Todd tells Joe that the contract is "permanent" (for life), but how does Joe see it?

4. What does Joe feel just before he signs the contract?

5. Why was Brad surprised to see Joe investing in copper?

6. What does Bonnie want Joe to do before she will marry him?

7. What does Joe plan to do while he is away from work?

a. Joe now has expensive clothes and a new sports car.

b. terror

c. have some big parties

d. Prices had been going down.

e. He thinks he can get out of it later on.

f. Top people usually have officers higher up in a building.

g. quit working

B. **For each statement, write who or what the words in italics refer to.**

1. *He* had not made an appointment. (page 28) _____

2. "I like to control *it* from here." (page 30) _____

3. "I'm sorry—I'm too used to *them*." (page 30) _____

4. *It* was full of things requiring you to work for them and nobody else. (page 33) _____

5. "I don't suppose he liked *that* one bit." (page 36) _____

6. "*It* was held in his new apartment." (page 46) _____

7. ". . . *it's* going to be perfect." (page 47) _____

C. **Complete the summary with the words from the box.**

two hundred	promotion	control	money
twentieth	Riverside	Bonnie	three
wood	Brad	books	blood
promoted	Don Smitty	cigar	copper

Todd's office was small and full of dark **1.** _____ and old **2.** _____. Todd asked Joe if his **3.** _____ bothered him. He told Joe that the company was going to give him a **4.** _____. Joe wanted to have **5.** _____ over **6.** _____ more than anything else. He signed the contract in his own **7.** _____. When he returned to his office **8.** _____ told Joe he had been **9.** _____. His new office was on the **10.** _____ floor and had once belonged to **11.** _____. Joe then invested in **12.** _____ shares and made a lot of money. He bought a new apartment on **13.** _____ and showed it to **14.** _____. He took time off work and planned **15.** _____ big parties. At the first he invited **16.** _____ people.

Review: Chapters 8–10

A. Read this summary of part of the story. Six mistakes have been underlined. Rewrite the summary, correcting the mistakes.

At Joe's <u>second</u> party Bonnie arrived with <u>Brad Benson</u>. Joe learned that Dawson Coles had left the company and wanted to use his money to invest in things that would <u>make a lot of money</u>. Later, Joe waits to meet Bonnie at <u>Macey's Bar</u>. Rey Todd arrives and tells Joe to <u>take a longer holiday</u>. Todd leaves and Bonnie comes in. They argue and Bonnie slaps his face because <u>he refuses to marry her</u>.

B. Number these events in the order they happened (1 to 6).

Bonnie finishes with Joe.   _____

Joe invests in copper.   _____

Joe invests in new electrical developments.   _____

Joe sees Rey Todd at his party.   _____

Todd interviews Sam Lazlo.   _____

Joe is photographed with an actress.   _____

Joe takes his new car to the Bronx.   _____

C. Complete the crossword puzzle using the clues below.

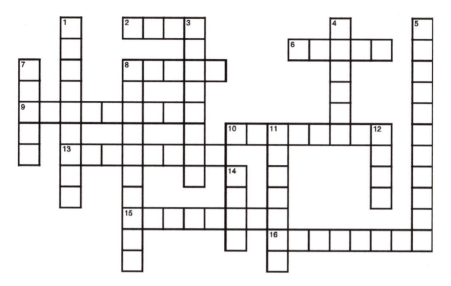

Across

2. to stop or finish something

6. The name of Joe's girlfriend is Bonnie _____.

8. Joe signed his contract in his own _____.

9. These are people who have a college degree.

10. An aging film _____ tells reporters he is a friend of Joe.

13. Joe Faust comes from here.

15. He is interviewed at the end of the story.

16. Bonnie wore them around her neck at the party.

Down

1. _____ is the wealthy business center of New York City.

3. Joe's champagne costs one _____ dollars a bottle.

4. Todd tells Joe to make more of it.

5. He came to the party with Bonnie.

7. You can smoke one of these.

8. He used to be Joe's boss.

11. Joe thinks he isn't like him.

12. It's a red precious stone.

14. Joe likes this kind of music.

Answer Key

Chapters 1–4

A: **1.** g; **2.** a; **3.** f; **4.** d; **5.** c; **6.** b; **7.** e

B: **1.** T; **2.** F; **3.** F; **4.** T; **5.** T.

C: **1.** c, d, f; **2.** c

D: **1.** c; **2.** e; **3.** a; **4.** d; **5.** b

Chapters 5–7

A: **1.** f; **2.** a; **3.** e; **4.** b; **5.** d; **6.** g; **7.** c

B: **1.** Joe Faust; **2.** Rey Todd's office door; **3.** cigars;
4. Joe's contract with the company;
5. Joe's taking over the Investem Life Insurance account;
6. Joe's first party; **7.** Joe's third party

C: **1.** wood; **2.** books; **3.** cigar; **4.** promotion; **5.** control; **6.** money;
7. blood; **8.** Brad; **9.** promoted; **10.** twentieth; **11.** Don Smitty;
12. copper; **13.** Riverside; **14.** Bonnie; **15.** three;
16. two hundred

Chapters 8–10

At Joe's third party Bonnie arrived with Dawson Coles. Joe learned that
Dawson Coles had left the company and wanted to use his money to invest
in things that would help the planet. Later, Joe waits to meet Bonnie at the
hotel café. Rey Todd arrives and tells Joe to return to work. Todd leaves
and Bonnie comes in. They argue and Bonnie slaps his face because she
saw the newspaper story about Joe and the actress.

B: 2; 6; 4; 1; 7; 3; 5

C: **Across:** **2.** quit; **6.** Perez; **8.** blood; **9.** graduates; **10.** director;
13. The Bronx; **15.** Sam Lazlo; **16.** diamonds

Down: **1.** Manhattan; **3.** thousand; **4.** profit; **5.** Dawson Coles;
7. cigar; **8.** Brad Benson; **11.** Rey Todd; **12.** Ruby;
14. jazz

Background Reading:

Spotlight on ... *New York City*

Read the information about New York City and answer the questions below.

New York City, in the state of New York, is the largest city in the USA. Manhattan is an area of New York City that includes important centers of business. Property in some of the wealthier parts of Manhattan, such as the business districts, can be very expensive.

The Bronx is another area in New York City and has a high population. Some of the poorer parts of the Bronx, such as the South Bronx, have had social problems and high levels of crime in the past, though recent times have seen many improvements.

Manhattan and the Bronx have been featured in many Hollywood movies. These movies have often presented Manhattan as being mostly wealthy and the Bronx as very poor. In real life there are rich and poor areas in both places.

1. What part of New York do you think Dawson Coles might choose to live in and why?

2. What part of New York do you think Joe Faust came from? Why do you think he wanted to leave it?

3. Many cities in the world have social problems. Name any cities you know that have social problems and explain what these problems are.

Background Reading:

Spotlight on . . . *Faust*

A. Joe Faust is based on one of several stories about an earlier character named Faust. Read the account of one version of this story and answer the questions below.

A long time ago there was a professor called John Faust. He was so clever that he had learned everything that his university could teach him. He became bored and wanted new things to learn and new experiences to have. He decided that the only way he could do this was to sell his soul to the devil in exchange for knowledge and power. The Devil, hungry to have Faust's soul, made Faust sign a contract in his own blood. This contract stated that Faust would have great power and knowledge, but after twenty years his soul would be claimed by the devil, and then Faust would go to

Rembrandt van Rijn - FAUST

Hell. A demon called Mephistopheles served Faust for all this time, but Faust wasted his power on unimportant things. He didn't find satisfaction or happiness. When the end of his contract came, Faust was too proud to ask God for forgiveness, even though he would have saved his soul if he had done so. At the end of the twenty years of Faust's contract, Mephistopheles came and took Faust's soul to Hell.

(Retold by Frank Brennan)

1. Write down ways in which the stories about Joe Faust and John Faust are alike and ways in which they are different.

2. What are some advantages and disadvantages of signing a job contract for life? Make a list.

B. Answer the questions below.

1. Can you think of any famous people from the past or present whose stories remind you of John Faust or Joe Faust? If so, why did you choose them?

2. "Joe Faust" is set in the world of modern business. Why do you think the business world was chosen for this story?

3. Do you think "Joe Faust" should have a happier ending? If so, suggest a happier ending to the story. If not, say why you prefer it the way it is.

4. In this story Joe Faust has the opportunity to use his money in many ways. Look at this list of things that money can or can't buy for him. Which do you think money CAN buy (✔), and which do you think it CAN'T (✘)?

good friends   _____

happiness   _____

expensive cars and clothes   _____

freedom   _____

holidays   _____

job satisfaction   _____

love   _____

a way to help other people   _____

respect   _____

fame   _____

Glossary

betrayal	(*n.*)	actions to hurt or disappoint someone who loves or trusts you
bittersweet	(*adj.*)	mixed feelings of being happy but sad about the same event
bonus	(*n.*)	an amount of money given in addition to salary
charity	(*n.*)	an institution that helps the poor
cigar	(*n.*)	a small roll of tobacco for smoking
cologne	(*n.*)	a light perfume for men
convertible	(*n.*)	a car with a soft roof that can be folded down
copper	(*n.*)	an orange-red metal
director	(*n.*)	a person who makes movies
exclusive	(*adj.*)	a news story reported by only one source
graduate	(*n.*)	a person who holds a degree from a university
jazz	(*n.*)	American music that came from ragtime and blues
profitable	(*adj.*)	making money
quit	(*v.*)	end your job
ruby	(*n.*)	a precious red stone
soul	(*n.*)	a person's total self; spirit
sum	(*n.*)	the whole amount
terminal	(*n.*)	the place passengers get on and off planes at the airport
tin	(*n.*)	a silver-colored metal